HORSE WOMEN

HORSEWOMEN

STRENGTH BEAUTY PASSION

WILLOW CREEK PRESS

For my favorite horse woman, my mother

For their contributions, a special thanks to
Kim McElroy www.spiritofhorse.com
Jennifer Grais www.spirithorsemedicine.com
Trish Broersma www.greenhorsegraphics.com

Published by Willow Creek Press, P.O. Box 147, Minocqua, Wisconsin 54548
Compiled by Melissa Sovey; designed by Donnie Rubo

Photo credits: p2,5,7 © Archiv Boiselle/ Gabriele Boiselle; p8,11 © Londie G. Padelsky; p12-15 © Denver Bryan/denverbryan.com; p16,17 © Archiv Boiselle/ Gabriele Boiselle; p18 © Dusty L. Perin; p19-21,23,24 © Sabine Stuewer; p26,27 © Archiv Boiselle/ Gabriele Boiselle; p29,30 © Sabine Stuewer; p33 © Dusty L. Perin; p34 © Archiv Boiselle/ Gabriele Boiselle; p36,37 © Archiv Boiselle/ Gabriele Boiselle; p38 © Ron Kimball/ ronkimballstock.com; p39 © Archiv Boiselle/ Gabriele Boiselle; p40 © Sabine Stuewer; p42-44 © Dusty L. Perin; p45 © Ron Kimball/ ronkimballstock.com; p46 © Archiv Boiselle/ Gabriele Boiselle; p47 © Ron Kimball/ ronkimballstock.com; p48,49 © Dusty L. Perin; p50,51 © Archiv Boiselle/ Gabriele Boiselle; p52 © Dusty L. Perin; p53 © Archiv Boiselle/ Gabriele Boiselle; p54 © Dusty L. Perin; p56 © Barbara Wright/ AnimalsAnimals; p57 © Sabine Stuewer; p59; © Archiv Boiselle/ Gabriele Boiselle; p60 © Robert Maier/ AnimalsAnimals; p61 © Jerry Cooke/ AnimalsAnimals; p62,64,65 © Dusty L. Perin; p66 © Archiv Boiselle/ Gabriele Boiselle; p67 © Ron Kimball/ ronkimballstock.com; p69-71 © Sabine Stuewer; p72,74 © Londie G. Padelsky; p75 © Ron Kimball/ ronkimballstock.com; p76 © Sabine Stuewer; p77-79 © Londie G. Padelsky; p80,81 © Archiv Boiselle/ Gabriele Boiselle; p82 © Londie G. Padelsky; p83 © Archiv Boiselle/ Gabriele Boiselle; p84 © Sabine Stuewer; p85 © Dusty L. Perin; 86,88 © Londie G. Padelsky; p89 © Dusty L. Perin; p90,91 © Londie G. Padelsky; p93 © Dusty L. Perin; p94,95 © Ron Kimball/ ronkimballstock.com; p96 © Londie G. Padelsky

Printed in Canada

As a woman bonds with a horse,
Attempts to understand and interpret...
she is nurturing, facing her fears,
and moving beyond boundaries.
Essential lessons in any relationship.

Then in this new, quiet communication
of touch and thought
intuition and expression...
she finds at last,
her Self.

- Kim McElroy -

I would stop for a moment as a young horse
riding out from the barn to gaze far across the open field.
Yearning far into the future that lay before us.

Then I eagerly carried you forward
away from day to day cares,
the hectic rush of the city
the square rationality of stall and barn and bale.
Into the breeze,
open fields of grass and gallops,
that clearing filled with a miracle of Monarch butterflies,
explorations into dark forests,
the joy of synchronous movement
opening the hearts of wounded souls
the Dance.
We gave one another all the gifts we have to
offer from our birthright —
you human
me horse.
We are bridge beings that way.

- Trish Broersma -

It is only rarely that
one can see in a little boy
the promise of a man,
but one can almost
always see in a little girl
the threat of a woman.

- *Alexandre Dumas* -

If I had influence with the good fairy
who is supposed to preside over the
christening of all children
I should ask that her gift
to each child in the world
be a sense of wonder so indestructible
that it would last throughout life,
as an unfailing antidote against the
boredom and disenchantments
of later years, the sterile preoccupation
with things that are artificial,
the alienation from
the sources of our strength.

- *Rachel Carson* -

There is only one big thing – desire.
And before it, when it is big, all is little.

- *Willa Cather* -

We have a hunger of the mind which asks for knowledge of all around us, and the more we gain, the more is our desire; the more we see, the more we are capable of seeing.

- Maria Mitchell -

Perhaps loving something is the only starting place
there is for making your life your own.

- Alice Koller -

Animals were once, for all of us, teachers. They instructed us in ways of being and perceiving that extended our imaginations, that were models for additional possibilities.

- *Joan McIntyre* -

It occurred to me when I was thirteen and wearing white gloves and Mary Janes and going to dancing school, that no one should have to dance backwards all their lives.

- *Jill Ruckelshaus* -

16

To me, horses and freedom are synonymous.

- Veryl Goodnight -

To those leaning on the sustaining infinite,
today is big with blessings.

- Mary Baker Eddy -

19

I am my own heroine.

- Marie Bashkirtseff -

*B*eautiful sisters, come high up to the strongest rocks,
we are all fighting women, heroines, horsewomen.

- *Edith Södergran* -

We are each other's reference
point at our turning points.

- Elizabeth Fishel -

Meanings, moods, the whole scale
of our inner experience, finds in
nature the "correspondences"
through which we may know
our boundless selves.

- Kathleen Raine -

I have noticed before that there is a category of acquaintanceship that is not friendship or business or romance, but speculation, fascination.

- Jane Smiley -

Like any art, the creation of self is both natural and seemingly impossible. It requires training as well as magic.

- Holly Near -

27

Each friend represents a world in us,
a world possibly not born until they
arrive, and it is only by this meeting
that a new world is born.

- Anaïs Nin -

Yes'm, old friends is always best,
'less you can catch a new one
that's fit to make an old one out of.

- *Sarah Orne Jewett* -

There is a space within sisterhood for likeness and difference, for the subtle differences that challenge and delight; there is space for disappointment – and surprise.

- *Christine Downing* -

I always felt that the great
high privilege, relief and
comfort of friendship was that
one had to explain nothing.

- Katherine Mansfield -

Silences make the real conversations between friends.

- Margaret Lee Runbeck -

When you hug
someone, you
learn something
else about them.
An important
something else.

- E.L. Konigsburg -

39

We are forever in the dark about what touch means to another... With touch, one enters at once a private and an ambiguous world.

- Jessamyn West -

This body of ours
has one fault:
the more you
indulge it, the
more things it
discovers to be
essential to it.
It is extraordinary
how it likes
being indulged.

- St. Teresa of Avila -

I generally avoid
temptation unless
I can't resist it.

- *Mae West* -

Lead me not into temptation; I can find the way myself.

- *Rita Mae Brown* -

Smell is the mute sense, the one without words.

- *Dianne Ackerman* -

Smell remembers and tells the future... Smell is home or loneliness. Confidence or betrayal.

- Cherrie Morage -

Acceptance is not submission; it is acknowledgement
of the facts of a situation. Then deciding
what you're going to do about it.

- *Kathleen Casey Theisen* -

There are two ways of meeting difficulties: you alter
the difficulties, or you alter yourself to meet them.

- *Phylis Bottome* -

Today I know that I cannot control the ocean tides.
I can only go with the flow... When I struggle and try
to organize the Atlantic to my specifications, I sink.
If I flail and thrash and growl and grumble, I go under.
But if I let go and float, I am borne aloft.

- Marie Stilkind -

Trouble is a sieve through which we sift our acquaintances.
Those too big to pass through are our friends.

- Arlene Francis -

To act without rapacity, to use knowledge with wisdom, to respect interdependence, to operate without hubris and greed are not simply moral imperatives. They are an accurate scientific description of the means of survival.

- Barbara Ward -

52

Kill the snake of doubt in your soul, crush the worms of fear
in your heart and mountains will move out of your way.

- *Kate Seredy* -

She listens to her own tales
Laughs at her own jokes and
Follows her own advice.

- Ama Ata Aidoo -

Long hair is considered bohemian, which may be why I grew it out, but I keep it long because I love the way it feels, part cloak, part fan, part mane, part security blanket.

- Marge Piercy -

Genius is an infinite
capacity for taking
life by the scruff
of the neck.

- Katherine Hepburn -

The natural world is dynamic. From the expanding universe
to the hair on a baby's head, nothing is the same
from now to the next moment.

- Helen Hoover -

When you were born
I held you wet and
unfolding, like a
butterfly newly born
from the chrysalis
of my body.

- *Joy Harjo* -

The events of childhood
do not pass but repeat
themselves like seasons
of the year.

- Eleanor Farjeon -

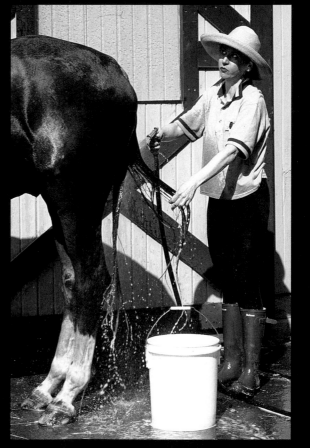

Eternally, woman spills herself away in driblets to the thirsty, seldom being allowed the time, the quiet, the peace, to let the pitcher fill up to the brim.

- Anne Morrow Lindbergh -

The solution for me, surely, is neither in total renunciation of the world, nor in total acceptance of it. I must find a balance somewhere, or an alternating rhythm between solitude and communion, between retreat and return. In my periods of retreat, perhaps I can learn something to carry back into my worldly life.

- Anne Morrow Lindbergh -

Even the most respectable
woman has a complete set of
clothes in her wardrobe ready
for a possible abduction.

- Satcha Guitry -

Absence is one of the most useful ingredients of family life,
and to do it rightly is an art like any other.

- Freya Stark -

I need no warrant for being, and no word of sanction upon my being. I am the warrant and the sanction.

- *Ayn Rand* -

Women have been taught
that, for us, the earth is flat,
and that if we venture out,
we will fall off the edge.
Some of us have ventured
out nevertheless, and so
far we have not fallen off.

- Andrea Dworkin -

We have only this moment, sparkling like a star
in our hand… and melting like a snowflake.
Let us use it before it is too late.

- Marie Beynon Ray -

Before you begin a thing remind yourself that difficulties and delays quite impossible to foresee are ahead… You can only see one thing clearly, and that is your goal. Form a mental vision of that and cling to it through thick and thin.

- Kathleen Norris -

If you let your fear of consequence prevent you from following your deepest instinct, your life will be safe, expedient and thin.

- Katherine Butler Hathaway -

$\mathcal{I}$'ll walk where my own nature would be leading;
it vexes me to choose another guide.

- *Emily Bronte* -

It isn't until you come to a spiritual understanding of who you are – not necessarily a religious feeling, but deep down, the spirit within – that you can begin to take control.

- Oprah Winfrey -

There is a passion for perfection which you rarely see fully developed, but… in successful lives it is never wholly lacking.

- *Bliss Carman* -

Our whole life is an attempt to discover when our spontaneity is whimsical, sentimental irresponsibility and when it is a valid expression of our deepest desires and values.

- Helen Merrell Lynd -

I'm the kind of woman that likes
to enjoy herself in peace.

- *Alice Walker* -

Inspiration does not come like a bolt, nor is it kinetic energy striving, but it comes to us slowly and quietly and all the time.

- Brenda Euland -

The woman who survives intact and happy must be at once tender and tough. She must have convinced herself, or be in the unending process of convincing herself, that she, her values, and her choices are important.

- *Maya Angelou* -

I gave my beauty and my youth to men. I am going
to give my wisdom and experience to animals.

- *Brigitte Bardot* -

Give us that grand word "woman" once again,
And let's have done with "lady"; one's a term
Full of fine force, strong, beautiful and firm,
Fit for the noblest use of tongue or pen;
And one's a word for lackeys.

- Ella Wheeler Wilcox -

The one important thing I have learned over the years is the difference between taking one's work seriously and taking one's self seriously. The first is imperative and the second is disastrous.

- *Margaret Fontey* -

Class is an aura of confidence that is being sure without being cocky. Class has nothing to do with money. Class never runs scared. It is self-discipline and self-knowledge. It's the sure-footedness that comes with having proved you can meet life.

- Ann Landers -

Years... should be nothing to you. Who asked you to count them or consider them? In the world of wild Nature, time is measured by seasons only – the bird does not know how old it is – the rose-tree does not count its birthdays

- Marie Corelli -

Thundering sky herd
of spirit horses
descending
hoofbeats, heartbeats
boom-boom!, boom, boom!
call of the world drum
bringing union
power
women and horses
dancing round the fire
birthing a new song
sing!
sing!
sing!

- Jennifer Grais -

You and your horse. His strength and beauty. Your knowledge
and patience and determination. And understanding. And love.
That's what fuses the two of you into this marvelous partnership
that makes you wonder, what can Heaven offer any
better than what you have here on earth?

- *Monica Dickens* -